DATE DUE

921
SHA

Murcia, Rebecca Thatcher
What it's . . . Shakira
(bilingual)

$18.50
BC#32457105002103

DATE DUE	BORROWER'S NAME
Dec 12	Jayden Hubbard
	Mia Va

921
SHA

BC#32457105002103 $18.50

Murcia, Rebecca Thatcher
What it's . . . Shakira
(bilingual)

Morrill ES
Chicago Public Schools
6011 S Rockwell St.
Chicago, IL 60629

What It's Like to Be...
Qué se siente al ser...

SHAKIRA

BY/POR
REBECCA THATCHER MURCIA

TRANSLATED BY/
TRADUCIDO POR
EIDA DE LA VEGA

Mitchell Lane
PUBLISHERS

P.O. Box 196
Hockessin, Delaware 19707
Visit us on the web: www.mitchelllane.com
Comments? email us:
mitchelllane@mitchelllane.com

Copyright © 2011 by Mitchell Lane Publishers. All rights reserved. No part of this book may be reproduced without written permission from the publisher. Printed and bound in the United States of America.

Printing   1   2   3   4   5   6   7   8   9

A LITTLE JAMIE BOOK

What It's Like to Be . . . Qué se siente al ser . . .

What It's Like to Be . . .	Qué se siente al ser . . .
America Ferrera	América Ferrera
The Jonas Brothers	Los Hermanos Jonas
Marta Vieira	MartaVieira
Miley Cyrus	Miley Cyrus
President Barack Obama	El presidente Barack Obama
Ryan Howard	Ryan Howard
Shakira	Shakira
Sonia Sotomayor	Sonia Sotomayor

Library of Congress Cataloging-in-Publication Data
Murcia, Rebecca Thatcher, 1962–
  What it's like to be Shakira = Que se siente al ser Shakira / by Rebecca Thatcher Murcia; translated by Eida de la Vega = por Rebecca Thatcher Murcia; traducido por Eida de la Vega.
    p. cm. — (A Little Jamie book = Un libro "Little Jamie")
  English and Spanish.
  Includes bibliographical references and index.
  ISBN 978-1-58415-851-6 (library bound)
  1. Shakira—Juvenile literature. 2. Singers—Latin America—Biography—Juvenile literature. I. Vega, Eida de la. II. Title.
  ML3930.S46M88 2010
  782.42164092 aB—dc22
                                                              2010006527

ABOUT THE AUTHOR: Rebecca Thatcher Murcia graduated from the University of Massachusetts at Amherst in 1986 and worked as a newspaper journalist in Massachusetts and Texas for 14 years. Thatcher Murcia, her two sons, and their dog live in Akron, Pennsylvania. They spent the 2007–2008 school year in La Mesa, a small town in the Colombian department of Cundinamarca. She is the author of many books for Mitchell Lane Publishers, including *Meet Our New Student from Colombia, Ronaldinho, What It's Like to Be Marta Vieira*, and *Dolores Huerta*.

ACERCA DE LA AUTORA: Rebecca Thatcher Murcia se graduó de la Universidad de Massachusetts en Amherst en 1986. Ha trabajado como periodista en Massachusetts y Texas durante 14 años. Thatcher Murcia vive con sus dos hijos y su perro en Akron, Pensilvania. Ellos pasaron el año escolar 2007-2008 en La Mesa, un pueblo de Colombia que está localizado en el departamento de Cundinamarca. Muchos de sus libros han sido publicados por Mitchell Lane Publishers, como *Meet Our New Student from Colombia, Ronaldinho, Qué se siente al ser Marta Vieira* y *Dolores Huerta*.

ABOUT THE TRANSLATOR: Eida de la Vega was born in Havana, Cuba, and now lives in New Jersey with her mother, her husband, and her two children. Eida has worked at Lectorum/Scholastic, and as editor of the magazine *Selecciones del Reader's Digest*.

ACERCA DE LA TRADUCTORA: Eida de la Vega nació en La Habana, Cuba, y ahora vive en Nueva Jersey con su madre, su esposo y sus dos hijos. Ha trabajado en Lectorum/Scholastic y, como editora, en la revista *Selecciones del Reader's Digest*.

                                                              PLB

Shakira is a singer and songwriter from South America. She was born in 1977 in Barranquilla, a city on the northern coast of Colombia. She is famous around the world because of her beautiful voice, her innovative music, and the way she dances on stage.

Shakira es una cantante y compositora de América del Sur. Nació en 1977 en Barranquilla, una ciudad en la costa norte de Colombia. Es famosa en todo el mundo por su hermosa voz, su música innovadora y el modo en que baila en el escenario.

SHAKIRA ISABEL MEBARAK RIPOLL

MICHELLE BACHELET,
PRESIDENT OF CHILE/
PRESIDENTA DE CHILE

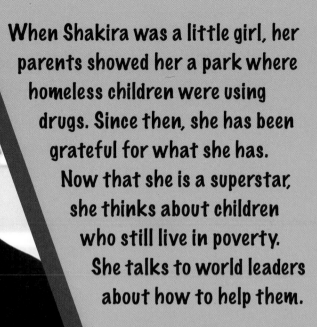

When Shakira was a little girl, her parents showed her a park where homeless children were using drugs. Since then, she has been grateful for what she has. Now that she is a superstar, she thinks about children who still live in poverty. She talks to world leaders about how to help them.

Cuando Shakira era una niña, sus padres le mostraron un parque donde había niños sin hogar que usaban drogas. Desde entonces, se siente muy agradecida por todo lo que tiene. Ahora que es una súper estrella, piensa en los niños que aún viven en la pobreza. Habla con líderes de todo el mundo acerca de cómo ayudar a los niños.

When she was nineteen, Shakira started the Barefoot Foundation. This group has built five schools in Colombia. They serve children who suffer from poverty and the civil war in their country. Shakira goes to the schools to talk to the children. She urges them to study—and to dance.

Cuando Shakira tenía diecinueve años, estableció la Fundación Pies Descalzos. Esta organización ha construido cinco escuelas en Colombia. Atiende a niños que sufren a causa de la pobreza y la guerra civil de su país. Shakira va a las escuelas para hablarles a los niños. Los anima a estudiar y a bailar.

Besides Colombia, Shakira has homes in Uruguay, the Bahamas, and Miami, Florida. She rides to work in a car or bus, just like millions of other people do. People try to take pictures of her wherever she goes. When she went to college in California, she disguised herself with a cap and a backpack.

Shakira tiene casas en Colombia, Uruguay, las Bahamas y Miami, Florida. Ella viaja en auto o en autobús, como lo hacen millones de personas. La gente trata de fotografiarla a dondequiera que va. Cuando fue a la universidad en California, se disfrazaba con una gorra y una mochila.

Shakira works with directors and musicians to record her music and to tape music videos. She writes most of her songs—in Spanish, English, and Portuguese. Sometimes she works with other songwriters, like Wyclef Jean. Together, they wrote the worldwide hit "Hips Don't Lie."

WYCLEF JEAN

Shakira trabaja con directores y músicos para grabar música y videos musicales. Ella se encarga de escribir la mayoría de las canciones: en español, inglés y portugués. A veces, trabaja con otros compositores como Wyclef Jean. Juntos escribieron el éxito internacional "Hips Don't Lie".

Shakira's life is very busy. Along with helping children, writing music, and performing, she works out to stay in shape for dancing. She gets a lot of support from her parents, William and Nidia (top), and her longtime boyfriend, Antonio de la Rua (bottom).

Shakira tiene una vida muy ocupada. Además de ayudar a los niños, escribir música y actuar, hace ejercicio para mantenerse en forma para bailar. Sus padres, William y Nidia (arriba), y su novio desde hace diez años, Antonio de la Rúa (abajo), la apoyan muchísimo.

WILLIAM   SHAKIRA   NIDIA

ANTONIO & SHAKIRA

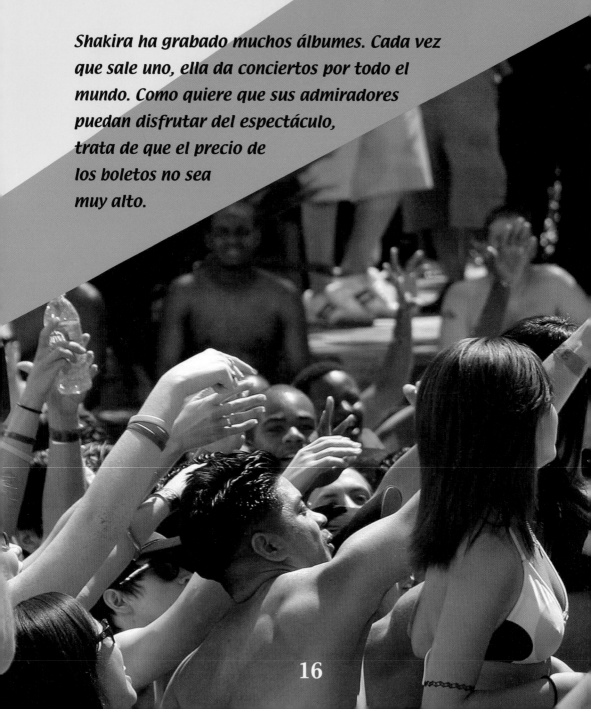

Shakira has recorded many albums. Each time a new one is released, she travels all over the world to perform in concerts. She wants her fans to be able to enjoy her shows, so she tries to keep the ticket prices low.

Shakira ha grabado muchos álbumes. Cada vez que sale uno, ella da conciertos por todo el mundo. Como quiere que sus admiradores puedan disfrutar del espectáculo, trata de que el precio de los boletos no sea muy alto.

During her tours, Shakira works with the United Nations Children's Fund. As a Goodwill Ambassador, she visits families that have been affected by disasters. In 2007, she visited victims of a cyclone in Bangladesh.

Durante sus giras, trabaja con el Fondo de las Naciones Unidas para la Infancia (UNICEF). Como embajadora de buena voluntad, visita a las familias que han sido afectadas por desastres. En 2007, visitó a las víctimas de un ciclón que asoló Bangladesh.

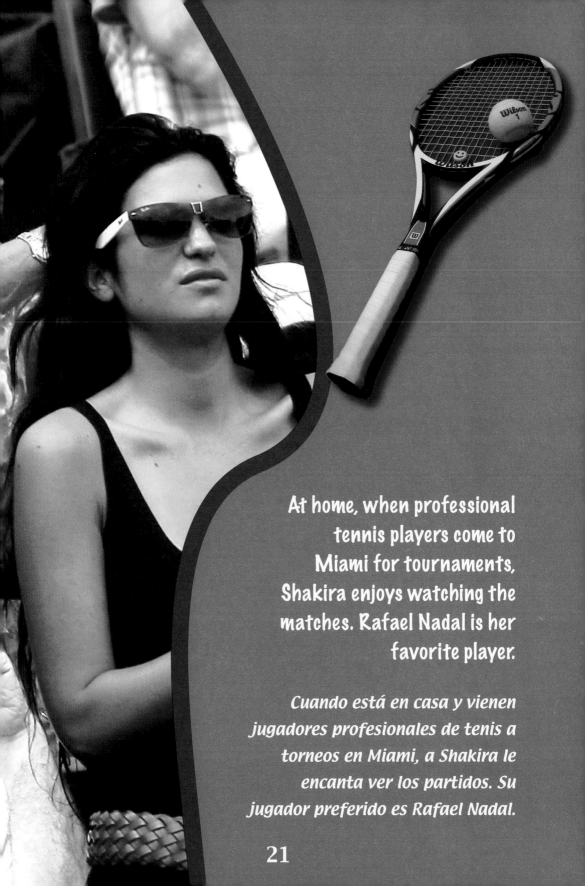

At home, when professional tennis players come to Miami for tournaments, Shakira enjoys watching the matches. Rafael Nadal is her favorite player.

Cuando está en casa y vienen jugadores profesionales de tenis a torneos en Miami, a Shakira le encanta ver los partidos. Su jugador preferido es Rafael Nadal.

Shakira loves animals. She often relaxes with Antonio at their farm in Uruguay. She hopes that one day she will be able to spend more time on a farm with her own children and a big garden.

UNITED STATES OF AMERICA
ESTADOS UNIDOS DE AMÉRICA

Colombia

South America
América del Sur

Uruguay

A Shakira le encantan los animales. Frecuentemente, se relaja con Antonio en su finca de Uruguay. Algún día espera poder pasar más tiempo con sus propios hijos en una finca con un jardín grande.

Shakira has dinner with other people in the music business. Amanda Ghost (left) is the head of Epic Records, and Sharon Dastur (right) works at a radio station in New York City. Shakira's favorite food is chocolate, but she also eats lots of vegetables, whole grains, and protein.

A veces, Shakira cena con gente del mundo de la música. Amanda Ghost (izquierda) es la directora de Epic Records, y Sharon Dastur (derecha) trabaja en una estación de radio en la ciudad de Nueva York. La comida favorita de Shakira es el chocolate, pero siempre come muchas verduras, granos integrales y proteína.

Although Shakira performs in huge stadiums for thousands and thousands of people, she is actually shy.

Aunque Shakira actúa en escenarios enormes frente a miles y miles de personas, es bastante tímida.

27

She puts her fears aside and gives a *muy caliente* concert!

¡Ella echa a un lado sus miedos y da un concierto bárbaro!

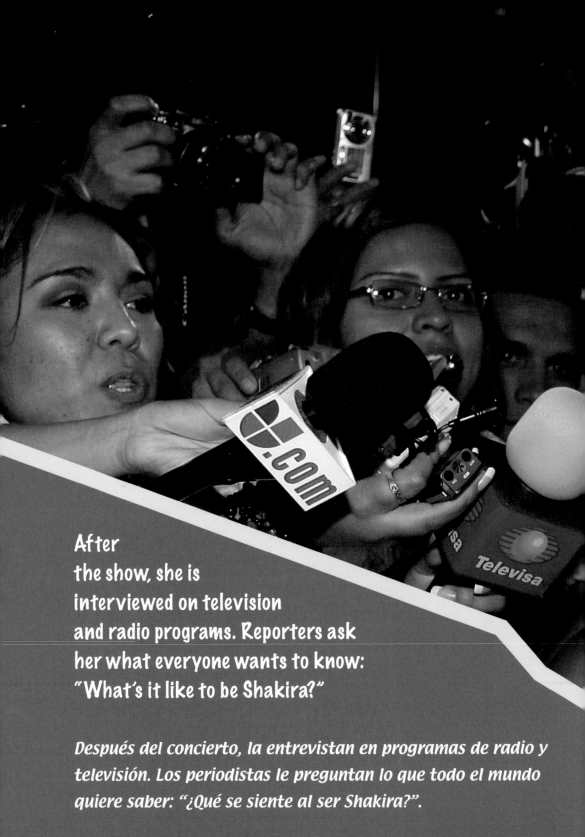

After
the show, she is
interviewed on television
and radio programs. Reporters ask
her what everyone wants to know:
"What's it like to be Shakira?"

Después del concierto, la entrevistan en programas de radio y televisión. Los periodistas le preguntan lo que todo el mundo quiere saber: "¿Qué se siente al ser Shakira?".

31

FURTHER READING/LECTURAS RECOMENDADAS

Works Consulted/Obras consultadas

Du Lac, J. Freedom. "In Any Language, A Whole Lotta Shakira Goin' On." *Washington Post*, August 31, 2006.

Ferguson, Euan. "The Making of Saint Shakira." *The [London] Observer*, November 22, 2009.

Gell, Aaron. "Love in the Time of Shakira." *Elle*, March 13, 2006.

"Home on Her Idyllic Uruguay Farm Shakira Talks Marriage and Kids." *Hello Magazine*, February 12, 2008. http://www.hellomagazine.com/music/2008/02/12/shakira-uruguay-farm/

Kimpel, Dan. "Shakira's Songs Are the Heart of Her Success." *BMI*, July 30, 2007; http://www.bmi.com/news/entry/535199

Malcolmson, Scott. "Shakira's Children." *New York Times Magazine*, June 2, 2009.

"Shakira Rests Hips to Study at UCLA," MSNBC, September 4, 2007. http://www.msnbc.msn.com/id/20768788/

"Shakira—Shakira Scores Most-Played Record." *Contact Music*, June 5, 2006. http://www.contactmusic.com/new/xmlfeed.nsf/story/shakira-scores-most-played-record_05_06_2006

"Shakira Visits Cyclone-Affected Areas and UNICEF Education Projects in Rural Bangladesh." UNICEF Press Release, December 19, 2007.

"Singer and Songwriter Shakira Appointed UNICEF Goodwill Ambassador." UNICEF Press Release.

Turner, Amy. "Shakira: Every Little Thing She Does Is Magic." *Sunday [London] Times*, March 1, 2009.

On the Internet

Alas the Movement
    www.alasthemovement.org

Shakira's Barefoot Foundation
    www.barefootfoundation.com

Shakira's Official Website
    www.shakira.com

United Nations Children's Fund
    www.unicef.org

En Internet

La Fundación Pies Descalzos de Shakira
    www.fundacionpiesdescalzos.com

La Página Oficial de Shakira
    es.shakira.com

Movimiento Alas
    www.movimientoalas.org

UNICEF en Español
    www.unicef.org/spanish

INDEX/ÍNDICE

COVER DESIGN: Carly Peterson, Joe Rasemas. PHOTO CREDITS: Cover (left)—AP Photo/Stuart Ramson; cover (right)—AP Photo/Robert E/ Klein; p. 3—Ed Geller/Globe Photos; p. 4—AP Photo/Armando Franca;p. 7—Francisco Leong/AFP/Getty Images; p. 8—AP Photo/Luis Benavides; p. 9 (top)—Alberto Tamargo/Getty Images; p. 10—Jean Baptiste Lacroix/WireImage/Getty Images; p. 12—John Rogers/Getty Images; p. 14—Eric Bouvet/Getty Images; p. 15 (top)—Roberto Schmidt/AFP/Getty Images; pp. 15 (bottom), 29 (top), 30—Frank Micelotta/Getty Images; p. 16—Chris Polk/FilmMagic/Getty Images; p. 18—Shehzad Noorani/UNICEF viaGetty Images; p. 20—AP Photo/Pat Carter; p. 22—AP Photo; p. 24—Gabriela Maj/Getty Images; pp. 26, 28—AP Photo/Evan Agostini. Every effort has been made to locate all copyright holders of materials used in this book. Any errors or omissions will be corrected in future editions of the book.